Eggs

by Stephanie Schumacher
illustrated by Rick Brown

Harcourt

Orlando Boston Dallas Chicago San Diego

Visit *The Learning Site!*

www.harcourtschool.com

"Being ten isn't easy," Miya thought. She had so much homework to do.

She rushed into the house. Her mom was there with her best friend, Mrs. Phillips. Mrs. Phillips worked designing prostheses (pros•thḗsəs), which are devices to replace missing body parts. Miya's mom was a writer. The two friends enjoyed sharing their latest ideas.

Mom went to get some snacks.

"Miya," Mrs. Phillips whispered. "I can't wait for you to see the picture I painted for your mother's birthday."

"Oh no!" Miya thought to herself. "I've been so busy with projects at school that I've totally forgotten about Mom's birthday."

Not showing her worry, she politely said, "I can't wait to see your painting. I'm sure Mom will love it."

"I'll think about Mom's birthday later," Miya thought to herself as she went upstairs to work.

After school the next day, she talked to her brother, Tim, about what to do. Together, they decided to surprise Mom with a party.

There was lots of planning to do, but with Dad's help they figured out the time, the place, and the guest list. Miya would print the invitations because she could print very neatly and precisely.

"Let's bake a carrot cake for the party," Tim suggested, "because it's Mom's favorite." They agreed that their mother made the best carrot cake in the world, so they decided to use her recipe.

They were excited about their plan to surprise Mom. After all, Mom always surprised them with little treats, even when it wasn't anyone's birthday.

MOM'S
Birthday
Time: Saturday
at 4PM
Place: Miya and
Tim's house

Remember, it's
a surprise!

Nevertheless, they knew they couldn't surprise their mother if they baked in their own kitchen. They called Mrs. Phillips to ask if they could bake the cake at her house. That way, she could help them with the oven.

After they planned a time to go over, Tim and Miya searched through their mother's recipe box and found the one for carrot cake.

On Saturday morning, Mrs. Phillips called to invite Miya and Tim to watch a new video. Their mom said it was fine. As planned, Dad said he would take Mom out for lunch and a movie. That would allow Miya, Tim, and Mrs. Phillips time to get ready for the surprise party.

"Mrs. Phillips, you make the best cakes," Miya said as she plopped down on a chair.

Mrs. Phillips smiled. "Well, I really love to bake. I always modify a recipe by adding a secret ingredient or two. Then, I feel as if I'm inventing something new.

"When I'm cooking, I also pay attention to how I do things. That way I can figure out how to help people with disabilities do the same things," she continued.

"Then you can design devices that will help people do what they want to do," said Tim.

"That's right. Now, let's see that recipe," Mrs. Phillips said.

"I'm in charge of the icing!" Miya shouted. She had to make sure that was clear to Tim. "Icing is my favorite part of any cake. I like chocolate, vanilla, and peanut butter best."

"OK, then I'm in charge of the spices!" said Tim. "Spices make a cake smell good."

"Let's get started so we finish on time," said Mrs. Phillips, glancing at her watch. "The first thing to do is collect all the ingredients and measure them out."

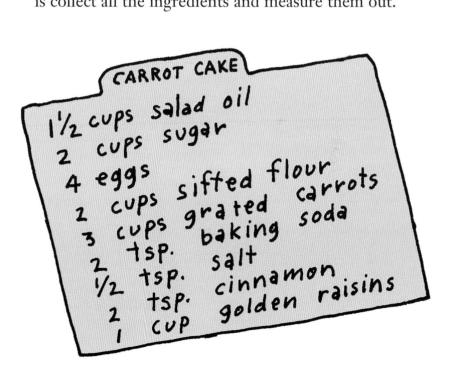

CARROT CAKE

1½ cups salad oil
2 cups sugar
4 eggs
2 cups sifted flour
3 cups grated carrots
2 tsp. baking soda
½ tsp. salt
2 tsp. cinnamon
1 cup golden raisins

Mrs. Phillips studied the recipe and read the list of ingredients aloud. They went from cupboard to cupboard collecting things. They took butter, eggs, and carrots from the refrigerator and put everything on the table. They also found measuring cups, measuring spoons, mixing bowls, and a pan.

Miya took out a paper and pencil and began to write.

"What's that for?" Mrs. Phillips asked.

"I like to document things as I go," Miya said. "If we add secret ingredients, I want to know what and how much. Then I'll remember what to do next time."

They measured out all the ingredients so each one would be ready when they needed it. Mrs. Phillips explained that part of being a good baker is being organized. She said that having all the ingredients ready helps you focus on the recipe.

"I see," said Miya. "That way you won't get distracted or confused."

Finally, Mrs. Phillips said they were ready. Miya began by beating the sugar and butter together. Mrs. Phillips reminded Tim and Miya that following every step in a recipe is important. As she cracked the eggs, Mrs. Phillips told them how she was especially proud of designing a prosthetic hand that allowed a chef client of hers to hold an egg without breaking it.

"Never forget the eggs," said Mrs. Phillips. "I did that once. What a disaster! It was the worst chocolate cake you could imagine!"

Tim added a little bit of flour at a time to the mixing bowl and stirred it in a circular motion, just as the recipe said.

Mrs. Phillips' son Billy came into the kitchen.
"What are you guys doing out here?" he asked them.

Tim smiled at him. "You're the smartest kid in
middle school, Billy. You figure it out."

"You even won a scholarship for science," added
Miya. "So guess why we're here."

Billy looked around and said, "You're baking a cake
for your mother's birthday."

They couldn't believe he knew it! How in the
world did he figure it out?

After all the ingredients were in the bowl, Mrs. Phillips announced that it was time for the secret ingredients. "What should they be?" she asked.

Tim and Miya knew it was an invitation for them to experiment. She told them to look in the cupboards and in the refrigerator to see what they could find.

Miya opened a cupboard and looked at the different cans, boxes, and bags. Then she found a bag of dried apricots and held it up.

"Is this a secret ingredient?" Miya asked, hopefully.

"It could be," said Mrs. Phillips.

Billy opened the refrigerator and held up a bag of potatoes.

"Is this a secret ingredient?" he asked. Then he added, "Just kidding."

Tim opened another cupboard and held up a bag of walnuts. "I think I have one," he called.

"It could be," said Mrs. Phillips.

Then Billy held up a jar of cinnamon. "I've got something that's perfect," he said. "Could this be a secret ingredient?"

"It could be," said his mother. "A pinch of cinnamon always goes a long way."

"Let's add lots of cinnamon!" said Miya. "Mom loves that spice."

Billy pulled something from the drawer. "What's this odd-looking device?" he asked, holding up something made of metal.

"It's a nut chopper," Tim said. "We can use it to chop the walnuts."

Everyone got busy chopping apricots and nuts. As each of them added a secret ingredient to the bowl, they mixed it into the batter.

Miya poured the batter into the pan. Then Mrs. Phillips placed the pan in the hot oven.

In about an hour, the smell of carrot cake filled the house. When the oven timer went off, the children rushed into the kitchen.

"Is it ready for the icing?" Billy asked.

"I'm in charge of the icing," Miya pointed out. "Maybe I'll let you help."

Mrs. Phillips set the cake on a wire rack to cool. It seemed like forever, but soon the cake was cool and they could frost it.

Once the cake was frosted, Mrs. Phillips brought out one more secret ingredient. The children watched as she rolled some marzipan candy into a ball. As she added drops of red and yellow food coloring, the colors mixed and turned the marzipan orange. Mrs. Phillips shaped it into a tiny carrot. Then she rolled another ball of marzipan. She colored it with green food coloring and shaped it into tiny leaves.

The children watched as Mrs. Phillips placed the tiny carrot on the cake. Then she gave each of the children some marzipan to make a carrot. One by one, they placed the finished carrots on the cake. It was perfect!

When Mom and Dad arrived home, the party was ready. Mom was truly surprised!

"I know this is my carrot cake recipe, but it's just a little different," she said. "Let me see. The apricots and walnuts are new, and I just love all the cinnamon spice. The carrots on top are adorable!"

"Mrs. Phillips always adds secret ingredients," Miya said to her mom. "We added some, too!"

"It tastes delicious!" Mom said. Then she turned to Mrs. Phillips and said, "Remember when we baked the chocolate cake and left out the eggs? What a disaster!"

The two of them started laughing. Mom was really having a happy birthday.